The new Solar System

Dwarf Planets

Robin Birch

CHELSEA
CLUBHOUSE
An Imprint of Chelsea House Publishers

Chelsea Clubhouse
An imprint of Chelsea House Publishers
132 West 31st Street
New York, NY 10001

Chelsea Clubhouse books are available at special discounts when purchased in bulk quantities for businesses, associations, institutions, or sales promotions. Please call our Special Sales Department in New York at (212) 967-8800 or (800) 322-8755.

You can find Chelsea Clubhouse on the World Wide Web at: http://www.chelseahouse.com

First published in 2004 by
MACMILLAN EDUCATION AUSTRALIA PTY LTD
15–19 Claremont Street, South Yarra, 3141

Visit our Web site at www.macmillan.com.au or go directly to www.macmillanlibrary.com.au

Associated companies and representatives throughout the world.

Copyright © Robin Birch 2004

Library of Congress Cataloging-in-Publication Data

Birch, Robin.
    Dwarf planets / Robin Birch. — 2nd ed.
    p. cm. — (The new solar system)
    Includes index.
    ISBN 978-1-60413-216-8
    1. Dwarf planets—Juvenile literature. I. Title.
    QB698.B57 2008
    523.4—dc22

                          2007051546

Edited by Erin Richards
Text and cover design by Cristina Neri, Canary Graphic Design
Page layout by Domenic Lauricella and Tony Carns
Photo research by Legend Images
Illustrations by Melissa Webb, Noisypics

Printed in the United States of America

Acknowledgements
The author and publisher are grateful to the following for permission to reproduce copyright material:

Front cover photo: computer artwork of dwarf planet Eris, courtesy of NASA, ESA, and A. Schaller (for STScI)

Photos courtesy of:
The Art Archive/Heraklion Museum/Dagli Orti, p. 14 (bottom); TSADO/NASA/Tom Stack/Auscape, p. 29; Chris Hellier/CORBIS, p. 20 (right); ESA/NASA/Dr R Albrecht, p. 21; Mary Evans Picture Library, pp. 8 (bottom), 24 (bottom); Walter Myers/www.arcadiastreet.com, pp. 5, 10, 12, 17, 18; NASA, ESA, and A. Feild (STScI), p. 11; NASA, ESA, and A. Schaller (for STScI), pp. 1, 3, 4, 6 (top), 24 (top), 28 (left), 30, 31; NASA, ESA, H. Weaver (JHU/APL), A. Stern (SwRI), and the HST Pluto Companion Search Team, p. 20 (left); NASA/JPL-Caltech, p. 13; NASA/Kim Shiflett, p. 28 (right); Photolibrary/Science Photo Library, p. 7; Photolibrary/Chris Butler/Science Photo Library, pp. 19, 22; Photolibrary/Mark Garlick/Science Photo Library, p. 4; Photolibrary/Roger Harris/Science Photo Library, p. 13 (left); Photolibrary/Detlev Van Ravenswaay/Science Photo Library, p. 6 (bottom); W. M. Keck Observatory, p. 27 (top); Sarah Anderson, W. M. Keck Observatory, p. 27 (bottom). Background and border images courtesy of Photodisc.

Please note
At the time of printing, the Internet addresses appearing in this book were correct. Owing to the dynamic nature of the Internet, however, we cannot guarantee that all these addresses will remain correct.

Contents

Planets and Dwarf Planets   4

The Solar System   6

Ceres   8

Pluto   14

Eris   24

Exploring Dwarf Planets   28

Dwarf Planets Fact Summary   30

Glossary   31

Index   32

Glossary words

When you see a word printed in bold, **like this**, you can look up its meaning in the glossary on page 31.

Planets and Dwarf Planets

There are eight planets in our skies. As well as the planets there are also dwarf planets.

The first three bodies to be called dwarf planets were Ceres, Pluto, and Eris. They are smaller than the eight planets, and became known as dwarf planets in 2006.

A planet is a body that:

- **orbits** the Sun
- is nearly round in shape
- has cleared the area around its orbit (its **gravity** is strong enough)

A dwarf planet is a body that:

- orbits the Sun
- is nearly round in shape
- has not cleared the area around its orbit (its gravity is not strong enough)
- is not a **moon**

> The word "planet" means "wanderer." **Stars** always make the same pattern in the sky. Planets and dwarf planets slowly change their location in the sky, compared to the stars around them. This is why planets were called "wanderers."

▶ An artist's impression of Ceres, the first dwarf planet to be discovered.

Ceres

Pluto

Eris

▲ The first solar system bodies to be called
dwarf planets were Ceres, Pluto, and Eris.

Ceres

Ceres was discovered in 1801. It was called a planet for about
50 years, as it is quite large. Then many more rocky bodies were
found nearby, and Ceres and the other rocky bodies all became
known as **asteroids**. Although Ceres is now called a dwarf
planet, it is still an asteroid.

Dwarf Planets Pluto and Eris

Pluto was discovered in 1930, and was called a planet until 2006.
Eris was discovered in 2005 and was found to be larger than
Pluto. Pluto was called a planet at that time, so **astronomers** had
to decide whether or not to call Eris another planet. They
decided to call both Eris and Pluto dwarf planets. Pluto and Eris
are known as **trans-Neptunian objects** as well as dwarf planets.

The Solar System

There are three types of objects revolving around the Sun. They are planets, dwarf planets, and **small solar system bodies**. All of these objects together with the Sun are called the solar system.

There are eight planets. Mercury, Venus, Earth, and Mars are made of rock. They are the smallest planets, and are closest to the Sun. Jupiter, Saturn, Uranus, and Neptune are made mainly of **gas** and liquid. They are the largest planets, and are farthest from the Sun.

Ceres, Pluto, and Eris are dwarf planets. Ceres orbits the Sun between Mars and Jupiter. Pluto orbits the Sun from about the same distance as Neptune's orbit, to farther out.

Eris orbits the Sun much farther out than Neptune.

▶ The solar system

There are many small solar system bodies in the solar system. These include asteroids, comets, trans-Neptunian objects, and other small bodies that have not been called dwarf planets.

Asteroids are made of rock. Most of them orbit the Sun in a path called the asteroid belt, between the orbits of Mars and Jupiter. Comets are made mainly of ice and rock. When they get close to the Sun, they grow a tail. Trans-Neptunian objects are icy, and orbit the Sun farther out than Neptune, on average.

► The eight planets are Mercury, Venus, Earth, Mars, Jupiter, Saturn, Uranus, and Neptune.

The solar system is about 4,600 million years old.

Planet	Average distance from Sun	
Mercury	35,960,000 miles	(57,910,000 kilometers)
Venus	67,190,000 miles	(108,200,000 kilometers)
Earth	92,900,000 miles	(149,600,000 kilometers)
Mars	141,550,000 miles	(227,940,000 kilometers)
Jupiter	483,340,000 miles	(778,330,000 kilometers)
Saturn	887,660,000 miles	(1,429,400,000 kilometers)
Uranus	1,782,880,000 miles	(2,870,990,000 kilometers)
Neptune	2,796,000,000 miles	(4,504,000,000 kilometers)

The name "solar system" comes from the word "Sol," the Latin name for the Sun.

Ceres is one of the first three bodies to be called a dwarf planet.

Discovering Ceres

The Italian astronomer Giuseppe Piazzi discovered Ceres on January 1, 1801. He was searching with a **telescope** for a star another astronomer had discovered. At first he thought Ceres was a comet because it looked like a star but moved in the sky. He observed it 24 times altogether.

No **space probe** has visited Ceres, either to land on it or study it up close. Many photographs have been taken of Ceres with the *Hubble Space Telescope*, and these tell us the little we know about its surface and what is inside.

▲This is the symbol for Ceres.

▼ The Roman goddess Ceres

Ceres was named after Ceres, the Roman goddess of growing plants and motherly love.

Ceres's Rotation and Revolution

Ceres **rotates** every nine hours around its **axis**. It rotates in an almost upright position.

It takes 4.6 Earth years for Ceres to **revolve** once around the Sun. This is the length of a year on Ceres. The Sun's gravity keeps Ceres revolving around it.

Ceres orbits the Sun between the orbits of Mars and Jupiter. When Ceres comes closest to Earth, it can be just bright enough to see with the unaided eye. We can see Ceres at this time if the sky is very clear and there is no human-made light or light from Earth's Moon in the sky.

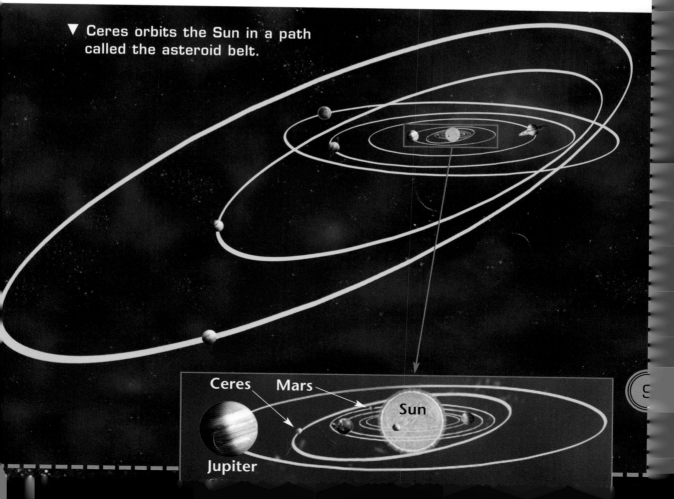

▼ Ceres orbits the Sun in a path called the asteroid belt.

Ceres   Mars

Sun

Jupiter

Ceres's Size and Structure

Ceres is 606 miles (975 kilometers) wide at the **equator** and 565 miles (909 kilometers) from top to bottom. It is not quite round in shape, as it is flattened at the top and bottom. Ceres is much smaller than any of the planets, and is smaller than Earth's Moon.

Ceres's gravity has pulled it into an almost-round shape. Ceres is large enough and heavy enough for it to have gravity this strong. This is one of the reasons Ceres has been called a dwarf planet rather than a small solar system body.

Earth

Ceres

Earth's Moon

▲ Ceres is much smaller than Earth's Moon.

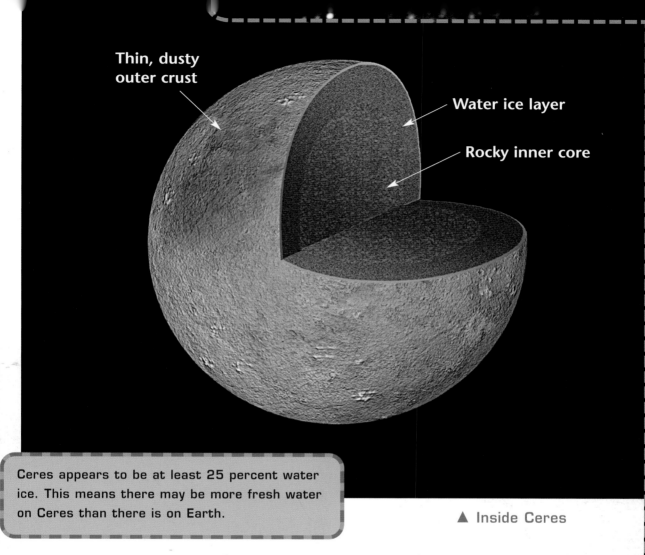

Thin, dusty outer crust

Water ice layer

Rocky inner core

Ceres appears to be at least 25 percent water ice. This means there may be more fresh water on Ceres than there is on Earth.

▲ Inside Ceres

For many years astronomers believed Ceres was just a ball of rock, with no layers inside it. Now some astronomers have discovered that Ceres may have a **core**, **mantle**, and **crust**, like many planets and moons.

Astronomers believe Ceres may have a large core of rock. This may be covered with a mantle, 37 to 75 miles (60 to 120 kilometers) thick, made mainly of frozen water with some ammonia. Astronomers also believe Ceres may have a thin, dusty crust on its surface.

Ceres's Surface and Atmosphere

Ceres probably has many **craters** on its surface. It orbits the Sun in an area where there are many other asteroids to collide with it. However, Ceres does not appear to have large, deep craters. They may have flattened out over time, from the movement of ice under the surface due to gravity.

Ceres may also have a very thin **atmosphere**. The average temperature on the surface of Ceres is –159 degrees Fahrenheit (–106 degrees Celsius). This is fairly warm for a body with little or no atmosphere.

Photographs of Ceres taken over the years have shown dark and light areas on the surface, which come and go. These markings may be soils, frosts, or craters.

▼ An artist's impression of the surface of Ceres

Asteroids

As Ceres revolves around the Sun, it shares its orbit with hundreds of thousands of other rocky bodies, called asteroids. The path these asteroids take around the Sun is known as the asteroid belt.

Many asteroids are only the size of pebbles. Twenty-six asteroids are larger than 124 miles (200 kilometers) across. Ceres is the largest asteroid, and the only one with an almost-round shape.

Ceres is called a dwarf planet because it shares its orbit with other asteroids. If Ceres were a lot larger, it would have stronger gravity. Then it may have gathered up, or pushed away, the other asteroids so there would be no other bodies near its orbit. If this were the case Ceres would probably be called a planet.

▼ Most asteroids are not round in shape.

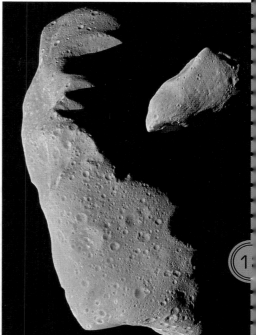

▼ An artist's impression of the asteroid belt. The bright star on the left is the Sun.

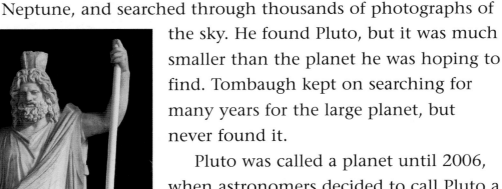

Pluto

Pluto is one of the first three bodies to be called a dwarf planet.

Discovering Pluto

Pluto was discovered in 1930 by Clyde Tombaugh. He was looking for a large planet farther out than Neptune, and searched through thousands of photographs of the sky. He found Pluto, but it was much smaller than the planet he was hoping to find. Tombaugh kept on searching for many years for the large planet, but never found it.

Pluto was called a planet until 2006, when astronomers decided to call Pluto a dwarf planet. Pluto is so small and far away we can only see it with a telescope. No space probe has visited Pluto to study it up close.

▲This is the symbol for Pluto.

◀ The Roman god Pluto

Pluto was named after Pluto, the Roman god of the underworld.

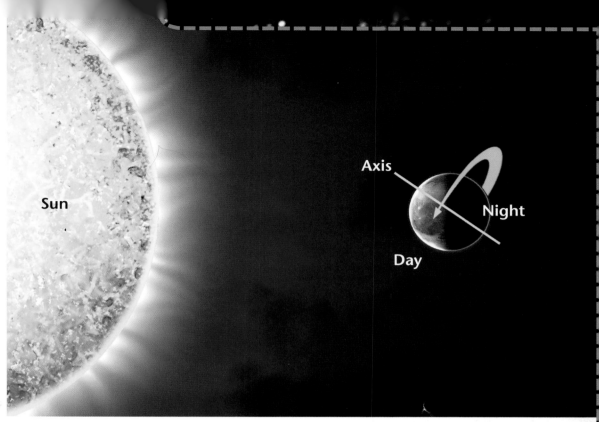

Sun

Axis

Night

Day

▲ Pluto rotates on its axis as it revolves around the Sun.

Pluto's Rotation and Revolution

Pluto rotates on its axis once every 6.4 Earth days. It rotates backward, compared to planet Earth.

Pluto revolves around the Sun once every 247.7 Earth years. This is the length of a year on Pluto. The Sun's gravity keeps Pluto revolving around it.

Pluto spins almost on its side as it revolves around the Sun. This means that when a **pole** is pointing towards the Sun, that pole has one long day, which lasts for many Earth years. When a pole is pointing away from the Sun, that pole has one long night. When the Sun is shining on the equator, a day and a night on Pluto take about six and a half Earth days.

Pluto's Unusual Orbit

Pluto revolves around the Sun in an elliptical, or oval-shaped, orbit. The Sun is not at the center of its orbit. When Pluto is closest to the Sun, it is 2,757 million miles (4,437 million kilometers) from the Sun. When Pluto is farthest from the Sun, it is 4,583 million miles (7,376 million kilometers) from the Sun.

The planets orbit the Sun as though they are all on the same flat surface. We say that they orbit the Sun in the same **plane**. Pluto's orbit, however, is tilted compared to the orbits of the planets.

Pluto is known as a trans-Neptunian object because it orbits the Sun farther out than Neptune, on average.

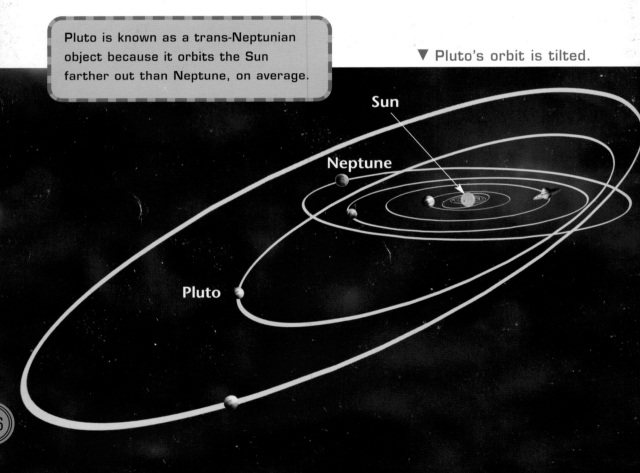

▼ Pluto's orbit is tilted.

Sun

Neptune

Pluto

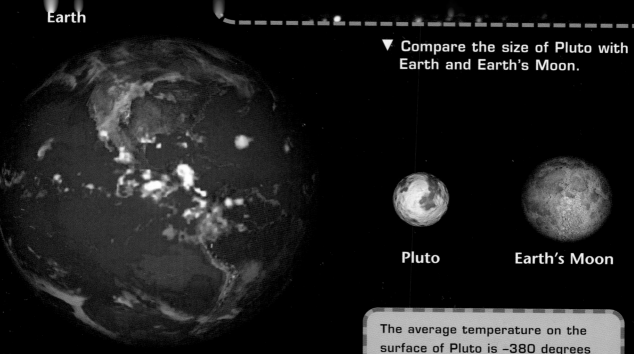

▼ Compare the size of Pluto with Earth and Earth's Moon.

Pluto   Earth's Moon

The average temperature on the surface of Pluto is –380 degrees Fahrenheit (–229 degrees Celsius).

Pluto's Size and Structure

Pluto's **diameter** is around 1,429 miles (2,300 kilometers). It is not large enough to have very strong gravity. Pluto's gravity is not strong enough to pull in, or push away, all the bodies near its orbit. This is why Pluto is called a dwarf planet rather than a planet.

Pluto is probably made of about 70 percent rock and 30 percent frozen water. It probably has ices on its surface, made mainly of nitrogen and methane. These ices form a shiny light brown layer on the surface of Pluto.

Pluto has bright areas at the north and south poles, and dark areas around the equator. The dark areas may be **basins** or craters made by rocks hitting Pluto. Or they may be frosts, which move about on the surface.

Pluto's Atmosphere

Not much is known about Pluto's atmosphere, but it probably consists mainly of nitrogen. There may also be small amounts of carbon monoxide and methane in the atmosphere.

Pluto's orbit takes it closer to the Sun and then farther away from the Sun. When Pluto moves closer to the Sun, its surface becomes warmer. Substances on the surface **evaporate**, making an atmosphere. When Pluto moves away from the Sun it gets colder. The substances in the atmosphere freeze and fall back down to the surface.

◀ An artist's impression of Pluto when it is closer to the Sun

▶ An artist's impression of Pluto when it is farther from the Sun

▲ An artist's impression of Pluto (in the foreground) and its moon Charon. Pluto's atmosphere can be seen as a haze on the planet's surface.

Pluto's atmosphere is very light and thin. However, it reaches higher up above the ground than Earth's atmosphere does. This is because Pluto has much weaker gravity than Earth. When Pluto has an atmosphere, some of it probably even escapes into space. Some of it may reach Pluto's moon, Charon.

Pluto's atmosphere is so thin that the sky would be black on Pluto and the stars would not twinkle. There would be no sound, because sound is carried by substances, such as air.

Pluto's Moons

Pluto has one large moon, Charon, and two tiny ones, called Nix and Hydra.

Discovering Pluto's Moons

Charon was discovered in 1978 by an American naval astronomer, Jim Christy. He was studying photographs of Pluto very closely to learn more about its position and orbit. He found a bulge on one side of Pluto, which turned out to be a large moon.

The tiny moons Nix and Hydra were discovered in 2005. They are only between 25 and 37 miles (40 and 60 kilometers) in diameter. Nix is about twice as far from Pluto as Charon. Hydra is about three times as far from Pluto as Charon.

▼ Charon the ferryman

Pluto

Nix

Hydra

Charon

▲ Pluto and its three moons

▲ This photo of Pluto and Charon was taken by the *Hubble Space Telescope*.

Pluto and Charon

Pluto and Charon could be thought of as partners, rather than dwarf planet and moon, because:

- Charon and Pluto are quite close together. They are only 12,204 miles (19,640 kilometers) apart, which is closer than Earth's Moon is to Earth.
- Charon is about half the width of Pluto. This is large for a moon when compared to the size of the body it revolves around.
- Pluto and Charon revolve around each other, instead of Charon revolving around Pluto.

Charon's Rotation and Revolution

Charon orbits Pluto in 6.4 Earth days. This is the same time Pluto takes to rotate once on its axis. Because of this, Charon is always in the same place above Pluto. So, if we could stand on Pluto, we would always see Charon in the same place in the sky. Charon would not rise and set like other moons in the solar system.

The same sides of Pluto and Charon always face each other. Therefore, if we could stand on Pluto, we would always see the same pattern on Charon. This is the same as the way we see Earth's Moon, with the same side always facing us.

▼ An artist's impression of how Charon looks from Pluto. The bright star on the right is the Sun.

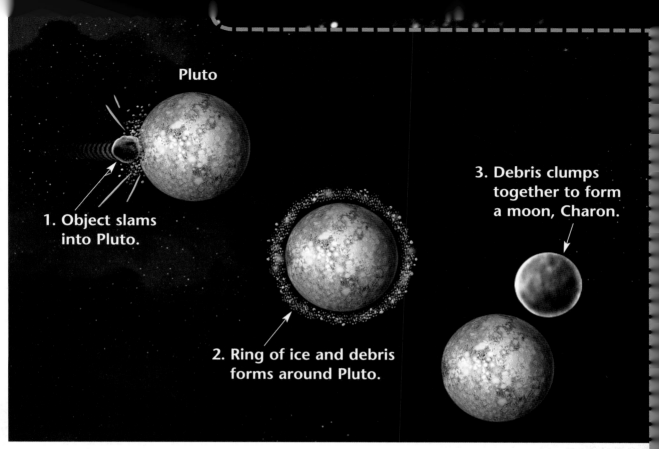

Pluto

1. Object slams into Pluto.

2. Ring of ice and debris forms around Pluto.

3. Debris clumps together to form a moon, Charon.

▲ The formation of Charon

Charon's Structure

Charon's diameter is 753 miles (1,212 kilometers). It is lightweight for its size, which means it would be made mostly of frozen water, probably with a small amount of rock. Charon's surface appears to be covered with water ice. The surface is a bluer color than the surface of Pluto.

Charon and Pluto are not made of the same amounts of rock and ice. This means they did not form together. Charon probably formed after Pluto had a huge collision with another body. The ice and rocky debris thrown up from the collision could have reformed to make Charon. The tiny moons Nix and Hydra are believed to have formed from the same collision that formed Charon.

Eris is one of the first three bodies to be called a dwarf planet.

Discovering Eris

Eris was discovered in 2005 by the astronomers Michael Brown, Chad Trujillo, and David Rabinowitz. They found it in photographs they had taken in 2003 with a telescope at Mount Palomar Observatory in Palomar Mountain, California.

▼ Eris, the Greek goddess

Eris was moving very slowly, which was why the astronomers did not notice it at first. When they discovered another slow-moving object, they decided to look back at their old photographs. This was when they found Eris. The astronomers kept watching it to figure out its orbit and size.

Eris is named after Eris, the Greek goddess of chaos and strife, because its discovery caused chaos among astronomers. At the time, they couldn't decide whether or not Eris was a planet.

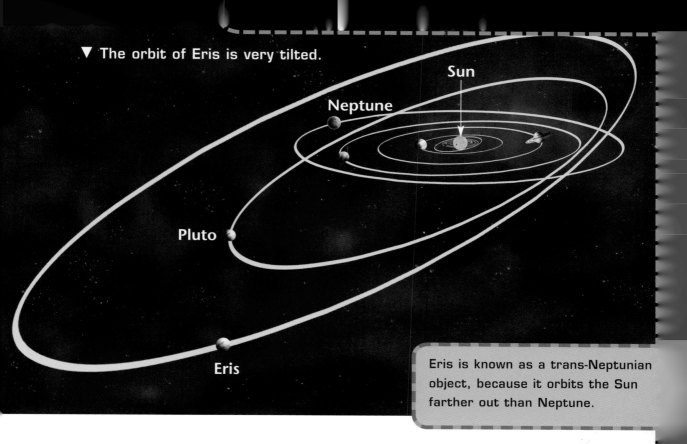

▼ The orbit of Eris is very tilted.

Sun

Neptune

Pluto

Eris

Eris is known as a trans-Neptunian object, because it orbits the Sun farther out than Neptune.

Eris's Rotation and Revolution

Eris rotates once on its axis in a little more than eight hours. This is the length of a day on Eris. Eris revolves around the Sun once every 556.7 Earth years. This is the length of one year on Eris. The Sun's gravity keeps Eris revolving around it.

Eris has an oval orbit that is very off-center. This means that Eris travels closer to the Sun, then farther away. When Eris is closest to the Sun, it is nearly one and a half times farther out than Neptune. When it is as far from the Sun as it can go, it is more than three times farther out than Neptune.

Eris's orbit is very tilted compared to the orbits of the planets. It is even more tilted than the orbit of dwarf planet Pluto.

Pluto

Eris

▲ Eris is more grayish in color than Pluto.

The temperature on Eris is around –405 degrees Fahrenheit (–243 degrees Celsius).

Eris's Size and Structure

Eris has a diameter of about 1,491 miles (2,400 kilometers). It is large enough for its gravity to pull it into an almost-round shape. This is why Eris is known as a dwarf planet and not a small solar system body. However, Eris's gravity is not strong enough for it to gather up, or push away, all the other objects in its orbit. This is why Eris is not called a planet.

Eris's Surface

Eris has frozen methane on its surface, like Pluto. However, Pluto is a light brown color while Eris is a gray color, probably because it is colder than Pluto. The frozen methane on Eris shows that it has always been very cold. That is because the methane would have evaporated otherwise. The methane could be coming from a reserve below the surface.

Eris's Moon

A team of astronomers led by Michael Brown discovered that Eris has a moon. They found it using a telescope with a **laser** guide system at the Keck Observatory in Hawaii. The moon has been named Dysnomia, after the daughter of the Greek goddess Eris. The name Dysnomia means "lawlessness."

Dysnomia has a diameter of between 186 and 249 miles (300 and 400 kilometers). It takes about 14 days to revolve around Eris. By observing Dysnomia, astronomers hope to learn more about Eris.

Dysnomia

Eris

▲ This photo of Eris and Dysnomia was taken at the Keck Observatory in Hawaii.

▼ Keck Observatory, Hawaii

Exploring Dwarf Planets

Astronomers are exploring space to find out more about the dwarf planets and the rest of the solar system.

There is a plan to send a space probe to Ceres and some other asteroids. The planned mission is called Dawn, and the probe should reach Ceres in 2015. It will orbit the asteroids it visits, and gather information about their structures, surfaces, and atmospheres.

A space probe is already on its way to Pluto and its moons, to study them more closely. The mission is called *New Horizons*, and the probe should reach Pluto in 2015. It will then fly on to visit other icy bodies farther out.

► The *New Horizons* space probe was launched in 2006.

▲ An artist's impression of a space probe visiting Pluto

Questions about Dwarf Planets

There are many unanswered questions about the dwarf planets
and their moons. One day astronomers hope to find out the
answers to questions such as these:

- Do Ceres and Eris have any atmosphere?
- What are the dark patches on Ceres and Pluto?
- Does Eris have dark patches on it?
- Do the surfaces of the dwarf planets have features such as
  mountains, valleys, and craters?
- Is there any movement on the surfaces of the dwarf planets,
  such as **volcanoes**?
- What are the dwarf planets and their moons really made of?

Dwarf Planets Fact Summary

	Ceres	Pluto	Eris
Average distance from Sun	257,070,600 miles	3,670,052,000 miles	6,344,199,800 miles
Diameter at equator	606 miles	1,430 miles	1,490 miles
Surface temperature	–159° Fahrenheit	–380° Fahrenheit	–405° Fahrenheit
Rotation on axis	9 Earth hours	6.4 Earth days	About 8 Earth hours
Revolution	4.6 Earth years	247.7 Earth years	556.7 Earth years
Number of moons	0	3	1

Web sites

 www.christinelavin.com/planetx.html
"Planet X"—a song about the discovery of Pluto

 www.nineplanets.org/
The eight planets—a tour of the solar system

 www.enchantedlearning.com
Enchanted Learning Web site—click on "Astronomy"

 www.solarsystem.nasa.gov/planets
NASA solar system exploration Web site

 www.solstation.com/stars/dwarfpla.htm
SolStation Web site—dwarf planets

Glossary

asteroids rocky bodies that orbit the Sun, and are smaller than planets

astronomers people who study stars, planets, and other bodies in space

atmosphere a layer of gas around a large body in space

axis an imaginary line through the middle of an object, from top to bottom

basins very large shallow bowl-shaped hollows in the ground

core the center, or middle part of a solar system body

craters bowl-shaped hollows in the ground

crust outside layer of a solar system body

diameter the distance across

equator an imaginary line around the middle of a globe

evaporate change from liquid to gas

gas a substance in which the particles are far apart, so they are not solid or liquid

gravity a force that pulls one body towards another

Hubble Space Telescope telescope in space that orbits Earth

laser a concentrated beam of light

mantle layer inside a solar system body between the core and the crust

moon a natural body which circles around a planet or dwarf planet

orbit *noun* the path a body takes when it moves around another body; *verb* travel on a path around another body in space

plane an imaginary flat surface

pole the top or bottom of a globe

revolve travel around another body

rotates spins

small solar system bodies solar system bodies which are not planets, dwarf planets, or the Sun

space probe a spacecraft that does not carry people

stars huge balls of glowing gas in space

telescope instrument for making objects look bigger and more detailed

trans-Neptunian objects bodies that orbit the Sun farther out on average than Neptune

volcanoes holes in the ground through which liquids flow

Index

A

ammonia 11
asteroids 5, 7, 12, 13, 28
astronomers 5, 11, 14, 24, 27, 28, 29
atmosphere 12, 18–19, 28, 29
axis 9, 15, 22, 25, 30

B

basins 17
Brown, Michael 24, 27

C

carbon monoxide 18
Ceres 4–5, 6, 8–13, 28, 29, 30
Charon 19, 20–23
Christy, Jim 20
comets 7, 8
craters 12, 17, 29

D

Dawn 28
day 15, 22, 25, 27, 30
Dysnomia 27

E

Earth 6–7, 9, 11, 17, 19, 21
equator 10, 15, 17, 30
Eris 4–5, 6, 24–27, 29, 30

F

frosts 12, 17

G

gas 6
gravity 4, 9, 10, 12, 13, 15, 17, 19, 25, 26

H

Hubble Space Telescope 8, 21
Hydra 20, 23

I

ice 7, 11, 12, 17, 23

L

liquid 6

M

methane 17, 18, 26
moon 4, 11, 19, 20–23, 27, 28, 29, 30
Moon (Earth's) 9, 10, 17, 21, 22
Mount Palomar Observatory 24
myths 20

N

New Horizons 28
night 15, 20
nitrogen 17, 18
Nix 20, 23

O

orbit 4, 6, 7, 9, 12, 13, 16–17, 18, 20, 22, 24, 25, 26, 28

P

Piazzi, Giuseppe 8
planets 4–5, 6–7, 10, 11, 15, 16, 25, 30
Pluto 4–5, 6, 14–23, 25, 26, 28, 29, 30
pole 15, 17

R

Rabinowitz, David 24
revolution 9, 15–16, 22, 25, 30
rotation 9, 15–16, 22, 25, 30

S

size 10, 13, 17, 21, 23, 24, 26
small solar system bodies 6–7, 10, 26
solar system 6–7, 22, 28, 30
sound 19
space probe 8, 14, 28
stars 4, 8, 19, 22
Sun 4, 6, 7, 9, 12, 13, 15, 16, 18, 22, 25, 30

T

telescope 8, 14, 21, 24, 27
temperature 12, 17, 26, 30
Tombaugh, Clyde 14
trans-Neptunian objects 5, 7, 16, 24, 25
Trujillo, Chad 24

W

water 11, 17, 23
Web sites 30

Y

year 9, 15, 25, 30